Worshipping God in the Digital Age

Worshipping God in the Digital Age

(Another View from the Pew)

Homer L. Isaac, Jr.

XULON PRESS

Xulon Press
2301 Lucien Way #415
Maitland, FL 32751
407.339.4217
www.xulonpress.com

Unless otherwise indicated, Scripture quotations taken
from the King James Version (KJV) – *public domain*.

Scripture quotations taken from the Holy Bible, New
International Version (NIV). Copyright © 1973, 1978,
1984, 2011 by Biblica, Inc.™. Used by permission. All
rights reserved.

Printed in the United States of America.

ISBN-13: 978-1-6305-0470-0

Dedication

This book is dedicated in loving memory of my mother, the late Bettie M. Douglas Isaac who loved God and reading the Bible. She always prayed for her children, worked and sacrificed everything to ensure that we all received a formal education before going back to school to complete her own education. Also, to the memory of my late father, Homer L. Isaac, Sr., who was always in church on Sundays and, in fact, died on a Sunday morning on his way to church.

Table of Contents

Introduction

The Digital Age, also referred to as the Information Age or Computer Age, is the historic period of the 21st centry in which God chose to bless humankind with the ability to harness knowledge in such a way that it could be easily accessed by anyone in our knowledge-thirsty, instant gratification society via an array of digital microminiaturized devices (see Glossary).

But what impact does this wealth of instantly assessable knowledge have on how we worship God and what does God expect from us? Certainly not less and biblically even more if we consider the scripture that says, "From everyone who has been given much, much will be demanded; and from the one who has been entrusted with much, much more will be asked" (Luke 12:48b). The answer then is not a simple "yes" that more is required, but, an emphatic "know" (pun intended)! That is to say that, the more we know about God, the more we know that we need to know more about God. Enhanced knowledge requires enhanced worship. Enhanced worship requires enhanced praise.

The Digital Age points us to fear God who alone is worthy of our worship because He cannot be understood by our knowledge, no matter how comprehensive we believe our knowledge to be. "The fear of the Lord is the beginning of wisdom; all who follow his precepts have good understanding. To him belongs eternal praise" (Psalm 111:10 NIV). "I, Wisdom, live together with good judgment. I know where to discover knowledge and discernment. All who fear the Lord will hate evil. Therefore, I hate pride and arrogance, corruption and perverse speech. Insight and strength are mine" (Proverbs 8:12-14 NLT).

The Digital Age has progressed so rapidly that the following story that went viral just six years ago, intended to be satirical, has become reality:

Subject: Church Services of the Future?

PASTOR: "Praise the Lord!" CONGREGATION: "Hallelujah!" PASTOR: "Will everyone please turn on their tablet, PC, iPad, Smartphone, and Kindle Bibles to 1 Cor 13:13. And please switch on your Bluetooth to download the sermon." P-a-u-s-e.......

"Now, let us pray committing this week into God's hands. Open your Apps, BBM, Twitter and

Facebook, and chat with God" S-i-l-e-n-c-e "As we take our Sunday tithes and offerings, please have your credit and debit cards ready." "You can log on to the church Wi-Fi using the password 'Lord909887. ' " The ushers will circulate mobile card swipe machines among the worshipers:

a. Those who prefer to make electronic fund transfers are directed to computers and laptops at the rear of the church.

b. Those who prefer to use iPad s can open them.

c. Those who prefer telephone banking, take out your cell phones to transfer your contributions to the church account. The holy atmosphere of the Church becomes truly electrified as ALL the smart phones, iPads, PCs and laptops beep and flicker!

Final Blessing and Closing Announcements:

a. This week's ministry cell meetings will be held on the various Facebook group pages where the usual group chatting takes place. Please log in and don't miss out.

b. Thursday's Bible study will be held live on Skype at 1900 hrs. GMT. Please don't miss out.

c. You can follow your Pastor on Twitter this weekend for Counselling and prayers. God bless you and have a nice day.[1]

The Digital Age has advanced so quickly that many of you are reading or listening to this book digitally. This rapid advancement suggests that we need to pause to examine the impact of this phenomenon on our worship. Using my anointed imagination, I envision this spiritual axiom:

"For every digital advancement that is positive for our worship; there is an equal and opposite negative temptation to impede our worship".

The apostle Paul said it this way, "So I find this law at work: Although I want to do good, evil is right there with me" (Romans 7:21). Use your digital devise to quickly look up a scripture and just as quickly a pop-up ad meets your sightline. Digitally look up the definition of a word and several un-related, but alluring articles appear. Yield to the temptation to take just a minute or so to check your e-mail or social media account, and a "breaking news" alert suspiciously shows up. And so on, and so on. Not to mention the ever-present temptation to play just one more digital game.

Scripture tells us to, "Be alert and of sober mind. Your enemy the devil prowls around like a roaring lion looking for someone to devour" (I Peter 5:8). Worshipping God in the Digital Age is a series of discussions with suggestions for avoiding impediments to digital age worship and offers ways to use our digital devices effectively to the glory of God. The book is written from the perspective of an ordinary pew worshipper.

Meditative Scriptures

From everyone who has been given much, much will be demanded; and from the one who has been entrusted with much, much more will be asked (Romans 12:48b).

The fear of the LORD is the beginning of wisdom; all who follow his precepts have good understanding. To him belongs eternal praise (Psalms 111:10).

So, I find this law at work: Although I want to do good, evil is right there with me (Romans 7:21). Be alert and of sober mind. Your enemy the devil prowls around like a roaring lion looking for someone to devour (Peter 5:8).

Technically, Moses was the first person with a tablet downloading data from the cloud.

Chapter One
Digital Bible Study

The Bible is the only book that you can never finish. It is alive! You will see new things each time you study it.

Q uestion: "Do I still need to study the Bible in the Digital Age?" The answer is: "Yes, more than ever". The more we know about God, the more we know that we need to know more about God. The Digital Age has just made it more convenient to learn so that we can know more. We no longer need to have several different bibles in several different translations at our disposal in order to study or to sarcastically be referred to as, "one of those bible-toting Christians".

There are several suggested plans available for reading the entire Bible in one year. These plans usually require reading a prescribed number of verses each day from both the Old and New

Testaments. Of course, reading the entire Bible is like the adage about eating an elephant, "How do you eat an elephant: one bite at a time". Like eating the proverbial elephant, it can be done but not with much enjoyment or any significant benefit. Eating is one thing, thoroughly digesting is quite another.

In the current 21st Century Digital Age we live in, we can now very easily "overeat" (consume too much information, or TMI) as a result of our easy access to the abundance of information available via our digital devices. Most of us have at least one digital device with at least one Bible app containing several translations of the Bible. Due to computer microminiaturization, we can now read our Bible on our digital devices practically anywhere and at most any time (and unfortunately most of us do, without regard or respect to time, place, location or situation).

Many years ago, while witnessing to a relative, who was obviously becoming very annoyed and defensive at what he perceived as my "holier-than-thou" boasting, asked me point- blankly, "Have you ever read the entire Bible from the beginning to the end?" Of course, I had not but I felt intimidated and concluded that I was not prepared to continue the conversation. I talked myself into believing that I needed to digest the entire Bible from cover to cover before I could be an effective witness. I was determined to "read" the entire Bible non-stop so that I would be ready to boast the next time I was confronted. Needless- to- say, I didn't retain much of anything. I simply read (I ate the whole elephant at one time!) in order to be able to boast that I had read the entire Bible.

I first started to seriously read (study) the Bible while working downtown in the seventies. A few blocks away was the local branch of the public library and I went there just about every day during my lunch hour. Having been raised reading only the King James Version of the Bible, I was absolutely amazed at the number of other translations and biblical reference books that were available. Parallel bibles were of particular interest to me, as well as, The Message, which proved to be exactly what I needed at that time in my spiritual development. As so well explained by the author, the late Eugene Peterson (1932-2018), in the Preface to the Reader: The Message is a reading Bible. It is not intended to replace the excellent study Bibles that are available.[2]

Another anointed spiritually imagined adage that comes to mind says:

"In the Digital Age we are living in, we often find ourselves swimming in an ocean of Biblical information yet drowning in a sea of spiritual ignorance".

Having digital resources available and not using them can easily make us lazy Christians. There was a time when, for example if you were driving a car and wanted to indicate that you were going to make a turn, you had to perform several functions in order to do so. First, you had to manually crank the window down so that you could give a hand signal while easing up on the clutch and simultaneously manually changing gears and turning the non-powered steering wheel. After that you were able to manually crank your window back up and then continue driving. Driving in the 21st century is much less complicated, and automobiles are standardly equipped with every imaginable convenience, such as, power windows, power steering and automatic transmissions yet we are generally less courteous now in indicating our turning intentions while driving. Not to mention distracted driving as a result of our addiction to our digital devices.

To avoid being labeled a lazy or ineffective Christians, we need to read, study and memorize enough relevant scripture, to use in any spiritual emergency. Spiritual emergencies are those unpredictable situations where our digital devices are either ineffective or fail at a moments' notice. These situations can include a discharged cell battery, no Wi-Fi signal, no internet access, an electrical grid down, hackers, terrorist attacks, global satellite interference and other unimaged events. And, of course, there is the occasional "senior moment" of forgetfulness.

Preparing for emergencies requires some prior thought, prayer and memorization. I have found that using the 26 letters in the alphabet to be a good tool for me to identify and memorize scripture. First, I use my digital device to identify a scripture that starts with the corresponding alphabet letter. If that verse or verses are personal or meaningful to me, I keep it, otherwise I continue my search until I find one that is personal or meaningful. When the list is complete, I try to memorize one verse a week until I have all 26 memorized. Of course, you can make as many different lists of alphabet scriptures as you would like if you have been blessed with that type of memory. Here's one of my lists (all KJV):

And be not conformed to this world: but be ye transformed by the renewing of your mind, that ye may prove what is that good, and acceptable, and perfect, will of God (Romans 12:2).

Bless the LORD, O my soul: and all that is within me, bless his holy name (Psalms 103:1).

Create in me a clean heart, O God; and renew a right spirit within me (Psalm 51:10).

Delight thyself also in the LORD: and he shall give thee the desires of thine heart (Psalm 37:4).

Enter into his gates with thanksgiving, and into his courts with praise be thankful unto him and bless his name (Psalm 100:4).

For all have sinned and come short of the glory of God (Romans 3:23).

God is our refuge and strength, a very present help in trouble (Psalms 46:1).

Hear, O Israel: The LORD our God is one LORD (Deuteronomy 6:4).

I was glad when they said unto me, let us go into the house of the Lord (Psalm 122:1).

Jesus said unto her, I am the resurrection, and the life (John 11:25a).

Know ye that the LORD he is God: it is he that hath made us, and not we ourselves; we are his people, and the sheep of his pasture (Psalm 100:3).

Let not your heart be troubled: ye believe in God, believe also in me (John 14:1).

Make a joyful noise unto God, all ye lands (Psalm 66:1).

No man can come to me, except the Father which hath sent me draw him: and I will raise him up at the last day (John 6:44).

O taste and see that the LORD is good: blessed is the man that trusteth in him (Psalm 34:8).

Pray without ceasing (1 Thessalonians 5:17).

Quench not the Spirit (1 Thessalonians 5:19).

Remember the sabbath day, to keep it holy (Exodus 20:8).

Sing unto him, sing psalms unto him, talk ye of all his wondrous works (1 Chronicles 16:9).

Trust in the LORD with all thine heart; and lean not unto thine own understanding (Proverbs 3:5).

Understand therefore this day, that the LORD thy God is he which over before thee (Deuteronomy 9:3a).

Verily I say unto you, all these things shall come upon this generation (Mathew 23:36).

Wait on the LORD be of good courage, and he shall strengthen thine heart: wait, I say, on the LORD (Psalm 27:14).

X Examine me, O LORD, and prove me; try my reins and my heart (Psalm 26:2).

Ye are the light of the world. A city that is set on a hill cannot be hid (Matthew 5:14).

Zacchaeus stood, and said unto the Lord: Behold, Lord, the half of my goods I give to the poor; and if I have taken anything from any man by false accusation, I restore him fourfold (Luke 19:8).

I invite you to take this alphabet scripture challenge:

FILL-IN YOUR PERSONAL ALPHABET SCRIPTURES

A

_____

_____

B

_____

_____

C

_____

D

_____

E

_____

F

_____

G

_____

H

_____

I

_____

J

_____

K

_____

L

M

N

O

P

Q

R

S

T

_____

U

_____

V

_____

W

_____

X

_____

Y

_____

Z

Once you have compiled your personal list, meditate on these three scriptures:

- ➤ Thy word have I hid in mine heart, that I might not sin against thee (Psalm 119:11).

- ➤ Thy word is a lamp unto my feet, and a light unto my path (Psalm 119:105).

- ➤ Study to shew thyself approved unto God, a workman that needeth not to be ashamed, rightly dividing the word of truth (2 Timothy 2:15).

Some people are hurting so
badly that you must do more
than preach a message to them.
You must be a message to them.

Chapter Two

Digital Scripture Verification

Don't take someone else's word for it. Read it for ***yourself****!*

The biblical tools available in the Digital Age provides us with the opportunity to easily, inspect, correct, reject or affirm as we reflect on God's Word. We don't need to simply take someone else's word; we must prayerfully read the Word for ourselves.

After working in the corporate world for several years, my wife Carolyn soon adopted the philosophical phrase, "trust but verify". This oxymoron was made famous by President Ronald Reagan who used it on several occasions in the context of nuclear disarmament discussions with the Soviet Union, according to Wikipedia. The purpose of digital scripture verification is not to cast doubt, but to identify scripture that could be more meaningful if it were scrutinized and clarified.

As a child in Sunday School at Williams Temple, I was taught at various times, by some well-meaning teachers who I thought, in retrospect, were honestly doing the very best they could, in their voluntary teaching roles, to impart God's word. But I have discovered that some of the things that were innocently taught incorrectly needed to be corrected or relearned.

In other cases, some scripture is intentionally being misquoted, or taken out of context for commercial purposes, and personal or financial gain. If we prayerfully use our digital devices, we can identify and correct any such scripture, as necessary.

"All scripture is given by inspiration of God, and is profitable for doctrine, for reproof, for correction, for instruction in righteousness" (2 Timothy 3:16).

One of the more common examples of scripture in need of further scrutiny often quoted is, "I can do all things through Christ which strengtheneth me" (Philippians 4:13), when quoted as a stand-alone verse. Often used as a stand-alone verse, this wording adorns many Christian products sold commercially. I would think those commercially sold items probably fall into the "best seller" category. Who would not want to believe that they could do all things? However, when we open our digital devices to Philippians 4:11-13 and parallel two other modern translations and read the stand-alone verse in context, this scripture is significantly clarified.

Philippians 4:11-13 King James Version (KJV)	Philippians 4:11-13 Living Bible (TLB)	Philippians 4:11-13 New International Version (NIV)
11 Not that I speak in respect of want: for I have learned, in whatsoever state I am, therewith to be content. **12** I know both how to be abased, and I know how to abound: everywhere and in all things, I am instructed both to be full and to be hungry, both to abound and to suffer need. **13** I can do all things through Christ which strengtheneth me.	**11** Not that I was ever in need, for I have learned how to get along happily whether I have much or little. **12** I know how to live on almost nothing or with everything. I have learned the secret of contentment in every situation, whether it be a full stomach or hunger, plenty or want; **13** for I can do everything God asks me to with the help of Christ who gives me the strength and power.	**11** I am not saying this because I am in need, for I have learned to be content whatever the circumstances. **12** I know what it is to be in need, and I know what it is to have plenty. I have learned the secret of being content in any and every situation, whether well fed or hungry, whether living in plenty or in want. **13** I can do all this through him who gives me strength.

As I look at these parallel verses, I believe I can do everything God is asking me to do. I can be content well fed or hungry; and live in plenty or in want, with the help of Christ who gives me the strength. But, no matter how much I would like to, I cannot do ALL things. The apostle Paul himself prayed three times requesting God to remove the thorn in his flesh concluding, each time he said, "My grace is all you need. My power works best in weakness." So now I am glad to boast about my weaknesses, so that the power of Christ can work through me (2 Corinthians 12:7 9 NLT). And Jesus prayed, "Father, if you are willing, please take this cup of suffering away from me. Yet I want your will to be done, not mine" (Luke 22:42 NLT).

Another scripture worthy of closer examination is Galatians 5:22 (NIV) "But the fruit of the Spirit is love, joy, peace, forbearance, kindness, goodness, faithfulness, gentleness and self- control". If you pull up this scripture on your digital device, you will see that 19 of the first 20 various translations reference *the* fruit. Those who read *the* fruit often go on to read the verse as though it reads the fruits (plural) of the Spirit "are" and then proceed to list them as if there is more than one fruit and we have a choice of which one is thought to be applicable to us. This is where there is a need for closer analysis. No matter how difficult it is for us to envision the fruit of the Spirit, it is composed of all these components, love, joy, peace, forbearance, kindness, goodness, faithfulness, gentleness and self-control.

My body is composed of my head, arms, legs, hands, feet, etc. But my head alone is not my body. It takes all these components to make my body just as the fruit of the Spirit is made up of all its' individual components. A cake recipe contains sugar, butter, eggs, flavor, baking powder, flour and milk. These ingredients combined make up a cake recipe, not just one or two of our choosing.

We don't ever want to fall into the trap that advertisers use in commercials. The use of the phrase, "up to 25% off" is designed for us to hear 25%, omitting the "up to". Of course, 1% is also up to 25%, but our minds tend to focus on what we want to hear, not what we hear.

The Word tells us that no weapon formed against me will prosper. We "hear" no weapon will be formed against me. The Word doesn't say no weapon will be formed. It says it will not prosper! "I have told you these things, so that in me you may have peace. In this world you will have trouble. But take heart! I have overcome the world" (John 16:33).

Studying scripture will keep us focused on what the Word is saying to us, and not necessarily what sounds good to us. We need to use our digital bible apps to, "trust but verify."

*Don't take someone else's word for it. Read it for **yourself**!*

Stop being impressed by people who can quote Scripture.

Be impressed by those that live Scripture!

Chapter Three

Opening the Doors of the Digital Church

I was glad when they said unto me, let us go into the house of the Lord (Psalm 122:1)

"A church that does not provoke any crisis, preach a gospel that does not unsettle, proclaim a word of God that does not touch the real sin of society in which it is being proclaimed: what kind of gospel is that?" - Oscar Romero (1917-1980)[3]

The story below involving a cell phone at church in the Digital Age says a lot about our 'church' attitude:

> *"His phone rang in church by accident during prayers. The pastor scolded him. The worshippers admonished him after prayers for interrupting the*

silence. His wife kept on lecturing him on his carelessness all the way home. You could see the shame, embarrassment and humiliation on his face. He never stepped foot in that church again. That evening he went to a bar. He was still nervous and trembling. He spilled his drink on the table by accident. The waiter apologized and gave him a napkin to clean himself. The janitor mopped the floor. The female manager offered him a complimentary drink. She also gave him a huge big hug and a kiss while saying, "Don't worry man. Who doesn't make mistakes?" He has never stopped going to that bar since then.[4]

Sometimes our attitude as believers drives others away from our church.

Traditionally after a sermon, the Shephard will extend an invitation to join the church, often referred to as an invitation to discipleship or "opening the doors of the church". In the Digital Age service begins when service ends, when the actual doors of the church are opened for dismissal after the Benediction.

Digital Age worshippers are not confined to brick and mortar buildings, although they regularly go there (usually at least weekly) to praise and worship God; to hear the preached word; to teach or be taught; to encourage others or be encouraged by others; and to fellowship face to face ("Blest be the tie that binds; Our hearts in Christian love; The fellowship our spirit finds; Is like to that above" -traditional hymn by John Fawcett).

Digital Age worshippers are reminded what is required when the doors are opened after weekly church service, " Each of you should use whatever gift you have received to serve others, as faithful stewards of God's grace in its various forms" (1 Peter 4:10).

So, in fact we are always the church, twenty-four hours a day, seven days a week, fifty-two weeks a year. "Do you not know that your bodies are temples of the Holy Spirit, who is in you, whom you have received from God? You are not your own" (I Corinthians 6:19).

An unknown author once stated, "I believe churches are meant for praising God. But so are 2 A.M. car rides, showers, coffee shops, the gym, conversations with friends, strangers, etc. Don't let a building confine your faith because we will never change the world just by going to church, we need to **be** the church." We must be careful how we live;

we could very well be the only Bible some people will ever read.

The digital devices that God has given to us are powerful tools to use for His service. Notice, for example how a visit with the sick or shut-in is now changed. A typical visitation used to consist of an inquiry about the persons current health, prayer and a scripture reading. Lastly, a halfhearted "If there is anything I can do, just call me" statement prior to departing. Now with our digital devices with us there are many opportunities to turn the sick visitation into a visit of service and compassion.

For even the Son of Man did not come to be served, but to serve, and to give his life as a ransom for many (Mark 10:45).

Here are just some of the things that are being done, or can be done when visiting the sick or shut-in in the Digital Age:

➢ During your conversation should you hear needs expressed, you can take care of many of those needs while you are talking or listening. If the person is hungry, you can send a text for a food order delivery and have it scheduled to arrive before you leave.

➢ If basic staples are needed, you could text an order to a grocery store for home delivery to the confined person or pick it up yourself and drop it off later. And if God has blessed you with the resources to be able to do so, you could pay for them yourself on your device as well.

➢ If the person is unable to cook, you can order a meal on your digital device for delivery while you are there. If they are lonely you could share the meal and fellowship with them.

➢ You can digitally share a sermon or music and listen to it with them.

➢ Order prescription medicine refills and pick them up from the drive-thru for them.

➢ Offer to process bill payments for them on-line.

➢ If there are un-attended chores to be done that require more than you can do alone, you can send a text to have another brother or sister to stop by to assist you or arrange a time when you can return to attend to them.

➢ Offer to digitally convert any media that they have been unable to enjoy because of their outdated electronic equipment.

➢ Help with internet issues, concerns or give operating instructions.

➢ Offer to make some phone calls for them.

➢ Demonstrate how to use features on their digital device that help with aging challenges that they may be experiencing, by setting electronic reminders for when and what time to take medications, calendar doctor's appointments and how to schedule transportation.

➢ Sit quietly, support and encourage as you listen to music on your digital device.

There are countless ways we can use our digital devices for sick visitation, but keep in mind the spiritual axiom:

"For every digital advancement that is positive for our worship; there is an equal and opposite negative reaction to impede our worship".

Beware of naysayers that point out that the sick or shut-in person has adult children that don't even visit them nor care for them, etc., etc. "Let their church members do it". "They are probably not really disabled, just lazy". "You could use this time to watch a movie or play a few games on your digital device."

Don't be discouraged by negative reactions. "So, let's not get tired of doing what is good. At just the right time we will reap a harvest of blessing if we don't give up" (Galatians 6:9).

"**11 So Christ himself gave the apostles, the prophets, the evangelists, the pastors and teachers, 12 to equip his people for works of service, so that the body of Christ may be built up 13 until we all reach unity in the faith and in the knowledge of the Son of God and become mature, attaining to the whole measure of the fullness of Christ. 14 Then we will no longer be infants, tossed back and forth by the waves, and blown here and there by every wind of teaching and by the cunning and craftiness of people in their deceitful scheming" (Ephesians 4:11-14).**

Don't judge someone just because they sin differently than you.

Chapter Four

Seven Suggested Digital Bookmarks

I would rather offend someone into heaven than to flatter them into hell.

The Digital Age has given rise to a host of digital preachers and teachers of their own "gospel". Some have become so proficient in memorizing and glamorizing someone else's sermon until it seems to be as good as, or better than the original. The low cost of digital technology and the emergence of social media have simplified streaming and pod-casting until you can listen to or watch a church service and have no idea if you are listening to a service from a store-front church or a mega-church service. Hand-held digital devices are as advanced, or more so, than their bulky predecessors with high definition broadcast and quality sound.

Many who have neglected to study the Scriptures have fallen prey to phony televangelists, sects and cults, believing everything they hear and then they try to convince the rest of us that what they have heard is true. Some are gullible enough to use their digital devices to send these 'churches' donations for blessings, prayer and healing.

Others will tell you 'exactly' when Christ will return, completely ignoring Matthew 24:36 "But about that day or hour no one knows, not even the angles in heaven, nor the Son, but only the Father". My book, *Worshipping God in an Imperfect Church* states it poetically this way:

They come from far, they come from near.
They will even prophesy that the Messiah is here.
They will tell you anything you would like to be true.
Bait you in and then drop the other shoe.
They are the ones who will leave you in a lurch
They are better known as the imposter church.

Rather than to argue against what these people have been taught or what they have learned in a "bible" that doesn't contain the word of God, we should be prepared to pull up our bookmarks from our digital device, the scriptures that support what we believe. Many people had never studied their bible prior to joining their newly found "our-way-or-the-highway religion". Some find it offensive when you try to share the Gospel with them. But I would rather offend someone into heaven than to flatter them into hell.

I strongly recommend that you bookmark the following scriptures in your digital bible so that you have them available for easy access at the opportune time.

John 3:17 "For God did not send his Son into the world to condemn the world, but to save the world through him."

Philippians 2:9-11 "Therefore God exalted him to the highest place and gave him the name that is above every name, 10 that at the name of Jesus every knee should bow, in heaven and on earth and under the earth, 11 and every tongue acknowledge that Jesus Christ is Lord, to the glory of God the Father."

2 John 1:9-11 "Anyone who runs ahead and does not continue in the teaching of Christ does not have God; whoever continues in the teaching has both the Father and the Son. 10 If anyone comes to you and does not bring this teaching, do not take them into your house or welcome them. 11 Anyone who welcomes them shares in their wicked work."

I have found that these seven verses address so much of the erroneous scriptures quoted by religious persons I encounter, that I have made a mental note of their location in the Bible, in addition to my bookmarks.

"Religious people will do what they are told no matter what is right; whereas spiritual people will do what is right, no matter what they are told."

From reading John 3:17, Philippians 2:11 and 2 John 1:9 for example, it is very clear that God wants His glory to come by way of His Son; to save the world and not to condemn the world. And those who don't continue in the teachings of Christ do not have God. This is not complicated at all. Yet there are countless religious people who are quick to tell me that Christ was not really God's Son, that there are certain sins that I must hate over other sins, and that I am not saved unless I do certain things, all because they were told those things by "someone". Sometimes that "someone" is one who is attempting to manipulate the minds of those too lazy to pull out their digital device and read the Word for themselves from their biblical app. What a shame to have the Word, the complete Word, with you and not read it!

Others try to bait us with prosperity theology, i.e., financial and physical blessings supposedly as a result of donations, as directed by their leaders.

15 Then he said to them, "Watch out! Be on your guard against all kinds of greed; life does not consist in an abundance of possessions" (Luke 12:15).

God has already blessed me far above anything I deserve or could ask. I am already financially and physically blessed with the things I have, and the difficult/challenging things I don't have.

If I were to place an imaginary value on my blessings or receive an imaginary credit on each one, and each blessing was valued at $1 million, I would easily be a millionaire just based on some of the blessings that I have right now and the challenges I have not had to endure because of God's mercy.

- ✓ No cancer. $1million
- ✓ Eyesight both eyes. $1million
- ✓ No amputations. $1million
- ✓ Mentally sound mind. $1million
- ✓ Ability to hear. $1million
- ✓ No paralysis. $1million
- ✓ Health insurance. $1million
- ✓ Disease free body. $1million
- ✓ Eternal life/salvation. PRICELESS

Scripture teaches us to, "Watch out for false prophets. They come to you in sheep's clothing, but inwardly they are ferocious wolves. 16 By their fruit you will recognize them. Do people pick grapes from thornbushes, or figs from thistles? 17 Likewise, every good tree bears good fruit, but a bad tree bears bad fruit. 18 A good tree cannot bear bad fruit, and a bad tree cannot bear good fruit. 19 Every tree that does not bear good fruit is cut down and thrown into the fire. 20 Thus, by their fruit you will recognize them" (Matthew 7:15-26).

Real shepherds are in it for the outcome, not the income.

Without judging anyone, we can use spiritual discernment to identify truth. Here are some examples.

- Prophet has a $5million jet plane. Is it used by the prophet to fly from one church to another only? Or is it also used to transport emergency aid to disaster victims or to provide transportation to the sick to specialized out-of-state hospitals?

- Religious leader has several expensive automobiles. Are they for show only? Or are they used to take the elderly and others needing transportation to the voting polls? Do they provide transportation to those that don't have the means to get to and from work or doctors' appointments, chemotherapy or dialysis treatment?

- Their religion shies away from any of those people who in their opinion are "different" yet created by God, because they do not sin the same way the members in their religion sin.

- Church has little or no involvement with feeding the hungry, providing for the homeless, standing up for injustice nor participates or gets involved social issues.

- The leader is only concerned about his/her church/denomination.
- Most of the church's income is allocated for salaries instead of church ministries.
- Major emphasis on collecting money with questionable or no or no accountability to the congregation.

I will not be fooled into believing false doctrine. Not only will I not listen to these false teachers, 2 John 1:10 gives me permission to "Shut the front door" and not listen to them. Verse 11 further makes me a co-enabler of this false teaching if I do let them into my home. I will not be a co-enabler!

"Not everyone who says to me, 'Lord, Lord,' will enter the kingdom of heaven, but only the one who does the will of my Father who is in heaven. 22 Many will say to me on that day, 'Lord, Lord, did we not prophesy in your name and in your name drive out demons and in your name perform many miracles?' 23 Then I will tell them plainly, 'I never knew you. Away from me, you evildoers!" (Matthew 7:21-23).

Jesus didn't say, "follow Christians".

He said, "follow me".

Chapter Five
Digital Dieting

When your words came, I ate them; they were my joy and my heart's delight, for I bear your name, Lord God Almighty (Jeremiah 15:16).

Your digital diet is what you digitally ingest. It is what you watch, what you listen to, what you read and the social media friends that you inter-face with. Be mindful of what digital food you are putting into your body emotionally, visually and spiritually.

In the Digital Age it is important that we maintain our spiritual health with a healthy digital diet. Like a nutritional food diet, we must be diligent in what we are ingesting and what we are communicating. Remember to start your day with your digital daily devotional reading and prayer in order to remain spiritually fit, being careful of what goes into and comes out the mouth of your spiritual body.

"Out of the same mouth come praise and cursing. My brothers and sisters, this should not be" (James 3:10).

An article written by Pope Francis entitled, "Do You Want to Fast This Lent?" provides some suggestions that are worthy of consideration for our digital diets in Lent and every season.

1. Fast from hurting words and say kind words.
2. Fast from sadness and be filled with gratitude.
3. Fast from anger and be filled with patience.
4. Fast from pessimism and be filled hope.
5. Fast from worries and have trust in God.
6. Fast from complaints and contemplate simplicity.
7. Fast from pressures and be prayerful.
8. Fast from bitterness and fill your hearts with joy.
9. Fast from selfishness and be compassionate to others.
10. Fast from grudges and be reconciled.
11. Fast from words and be silent so that you can listen.[5]

If we keep these suggestions in mind when we are communicating electronically or digitally, we will be less likely to wish we had not hit the "send" command, or the "post" command without first prayerfully re-thinking about our proposed action.

We don't want our best editing to be done **after** we hit the send/post button.

Mother Sarah Haygood (1928-2013) my former bible class teacher offered 25 things you can do to promote peaceful relations, most of which are applicable to our digital diet. Digital communications can lose compassion unless we continually promote peaceful relations. Here are some of her suggestions.

- Love yourself.
- Respect and value differences in others.
- Walk away from potentially violent situations.
- Say "Thank you".
- Be kinder than necessary and be there when people need you.
- Volunteer.
- Don't be afraid to say, "I'm sorry".
- Support.
- Tell how you feel about relevant issues.
- Be a good listener.
- Laugh!
- Make time to talk.
- Participate in your community of faith.
- Encourage peace at home.
- Live so that when others think of fairness, caring they think of you.
- Forgive yourself and others.
- Smile! - It's both free and contagious.

- Help a stranger.
- Take responsibility for your life.
- Know where your loved ones are and what is important to them.
- Provide protection and comfort to others.
- Encourage others to get involved in relevant activities that promote peace.
- Support victims' rights.
- Maintain a positive attitude.
- Turn the other cheek.

Do not let any unwholesome talk come out of your mouths, but only what is helpful for building others up according to their needs, that it may benefit those who listen. Ephesians 4:29

Chapter Six

Digital Tithing

The God who made the world and everything in it is the Lord of heaven and earth and does not live in temples built by human hands. 25 And he is not served by human hands, as if he needed anything. Rather, he himself gives everyone life and breath and everything else (Acts 17:24-25)

I have no need of a bull from your stall or of goats from your pens, 10 for every animal of the forest is mine, and the cattle on a thousand hills (Psalms 50:9-10).

Therefore, I urge you, brothers and sisters, in view of God's mercy, to offer your bodies as a living sacrifice, holy and pleasing to God—this is your true and proper worship (Romans 12:1).

Since God has everything and does not need any animal sacrifice, we can only offer as a living sacrifice our time as expressed as a digital tithe.

We can give Him back a tenth of our digital time, or a tenth of the time we spend with digital media.

It is estimated that in 2018 the average American spent 23.6 hours a week online or 5.9 hours a day.[6] So, we should be giving about 35 minutes of our digital down time to God, which still leaves us with over five hours of digital media time. Here are some suggested things we can do with our digital tithe:

1. Close our eyes and listen to God in silence.
2. Thank God for something He has done unexpectedly.
3. Say a little prayer for someone other than ourselves.
4. Pray for someone who has lost a loved one.
5. Thank God for protecting us from danger seen and unseen.
6. Think about Christ who died for our sins.
7. Spend a minute memorizing a new Bible verse.
8. Call someone who is sick, widowed or lonely.
9. Drop someone a card of encouragement.
10. Place some money in an envelope and mail it to a college student.
11. Pray for your church.
12. Say a prayer for your shepherd.
13. Make an alphabetized list of scriptures to memorize.

14. Thank God for what He has done.
15. Thank God for what He is doing.
16. Thank God for what He is able to do.
17. Thank God for undeserved blessings and mercy.
18. Pray for your family, relatives and friends.
19. Pray for your leadership.
20. Pray for those in the military.
21. Pray for the missionaries.
22. Pray for those that are incarcerated.
23. Pray for the mentally ill.
24. Pray for the homeless.
25. Pray for the country.

He says, "Be still, and know that I am God" (Psalm 46:10a).

Of course, there are times when we just need to put our digital devices down and remember that faith without works is dead. Cathy Peterson has said this:

When someone you know is going through a hard time, don't say, "call me if you need anything", rather say:

➤ *I'm doing grocery shopping today; send me your list and I'll drop yours off at your house on my way home.*
➤ *I'll pick up your kids for you; just let them and the school know who will be picking them up.*

> ➢ *I picked up some dinner for you; let me know the best time to drop it off.*
> ➢ *Let's have a cup of coffee tomorrow and talk. What time?*
> ➢ *I'm taking your kids to the movies so that you can have some "me" time.*
> ➢ *I'll be over to address thank-you cards later today.*
> ➢ *I'm off this Saturday so I'll be available for whatever you need me to do.*[7]

"When you pray, move your feet" -- African Proverb

"A new command I give you: Love one another. As I have loved you, so you must love one another. [35] By this everyone will know that you are my disciples, if you love one another" (John 13:34-35).

Chapter Seven

Deuteronomy 32:7 Digital Due Diligence

Remember the days of old; consider the generations long past. Ask your father and he will tell you, your elders, and they will explain to you (Deuteronomy 32:7).

Let this be written for a future generation, that a people not yet created may praise the LORD (PSALMS 102:18).

D igital technology also affords us the opportunity to comply with Deuteronomy 32:7 to "remember generations past." A generation is defined as all the people born, and living in the same time period, collectively. It is further defined generally as children that are born and become adults at about the age of thirty and begin to have children of their own. Current generally agreed generation names are:

- The Silent Generation: Born 1928-1945 (73-90 years old)
- Baby Boomers: Born 1946-1964 (54-72 years old)
- Generation X: Born 1965-1980 (38-53 years old)
- Millennials:1981-1996 (22-37 years old)
- Post-Millennials: 1997-Present (0-21 years old)

Regardless of the generation we belong to, we must be responsible with providing or handing down a written/digitized record of our ancestors, their faith and beliefs to our descendants. If there are any real or imaginary generational curses, when they say, "It runs in the family," this is the opportunity to say, "This is where it runs out."

Each member of the generations listed above can play a role in fulfilling this scripture. We must stop allowing the funeral director to unintentionally be our "Family Reunion Coordinator". Promises made at one funeral to see one another before the next funeral are often well intended but, these well intended promises are very seldom kept.

The Silent Generation

1. Encourage the younger generations to dig-itally record your story and memories of

your ancestors. Be sure to include stories of your faith.

2. Ask family members to digitize old photos for you so that they can be passed down through the years and last without fading.

3. Allow your family to take digital photos of the family record pages in your family bible in order to assist them with the development of the family tree.

Baby Boomers

1. Your generation is the 'squeezed generation', sandwiched between the generation that can provide the most valuable information and the generation that is the "me" generation, that usually has no interest in family history or genealogy. You must serve as the facilitator in coordinating this valuable family information. Ask anyone and everyone for their digital pictures of family members and download a picture of each family member into your data base.

2. Go on-line to the free U.S. Census records. Search and obtain every record applicable to your family. Add this information to your data base.

3. Collect any information already collected and researched by other family members

and merge their data into your database, after you have verified it.

4. Gather or take a digital photo of any family obituaries you don't already have. Pertinent information from these obituaries should be added to your database with a footnote indicating the source of the information.

5. Pair a family member of the Silent Generation with a family member from Generation X, the Millennial or Post-Millennial Generation and ask them to assist the elders with getting their story into digital format.

Generation X

1. Explain to your children the meaning of Psalm 102:18 as it relates to your family and how they can help to capture this information digitally.

2. Have your children search the internet for articles that pertain to your family.

Millennial and Post-Millennial

1. Ask your parents or grandparents to explain Deuteronomy 32:7 to you.

2. Ask them about their faith.

3. Help your parents or grandparents to learn as much about digital technology as patiently

as you can and how it can be used to pre-
serve family history for ensuing generations.
4. Learn all you can about your ancestors.

Personal digital devices have made it very easy to join into social media so that almost all family members can communicate individually or as a family with a family web site. All families will need someone to coordinate this effort. If you don't have such a person in your family, simply say, "Lord, here am I, send me," then do it.

There are several bible apps that your family can use on their digital devices that are readily available and are usually free. Many of these apps allow you to take notes, search keywords, and to participate in on-line group discussions in addition to the stan-dard digital bible functions. Every family member should have a biblical app on their digital device. If a family member doesn't know how to use their digital device, show them. "Each one, teach one".

We can remove flags and symbols all day.

But it's the hate in people's hearts that needs to be removed.

Chapter Eight

Starting a Digital Dialogue

*The fear of the LORD is the beginning of wisdom;
all who follow his precepts have good understanding. To him belongs eternal praise
(Psalm 111:10).*

*Nothing in all creation is hidden from God's sight.
Everything is uncovered and laid bare before
the eyes of him to whom we must give account
(Hebrews 4:13).*

Whenever a major or national event occurs that involves hate crimes or has racial overtones it seems to light a fire in the digital social media. Inevitably, someone will suggest that we need to have a conversation or dialogue about the subject. I do not disagree, however, in order to have meaningful dialogue there must be a common denominator among all participants. I suggest that the common denominator is God.

Without Him, any such conversation is futile as we would be attempting to reason with a fool.

Humorist Mark Twain famously quoted," Never argue with a fool; onlookers may not be able to tell the difference". Consider these verses in your Digital Bible:

- The fool says in his heart, "There is no God" (Psalm 14:1a).
- Stay away from a fool, for you will not find knowledge on their lips (Proverbs 14:7).
- The fear of the LORD is the beginning of wisdom; all who follow his precepts have good understanding. To him belongs eternal praise (Psalm 111:10).

The Southern Poverty Law Center has identified sixty-eight hate groups in the United States. The FBI tracks thirteen hate categories.[8] God sees all the activities of these groups, yet we still find reasons to hate.

In my opinion that indicates a separation from God. Since God is where God always has been, then we have moved away from God. God has not moved away from us. Therefore, unless we are holding a conversation with someone who does not believe in God (a fool), then any meaningful conversation must have God at the center.

If you agree, parallel John 1:1-3 on your digital device with the KJV and two other translations of your choice. Reading these verses, we should all conclude that God made everything.

John 1:1-3 King James Version (KJV) **1** In the beginning was the Word, and the Word was with God, and the Word was God. **2** The same was in the beginning with God. **3** All things were made by him; and without him was not any thing made that was made.	John 1:1-3 New International Version (NIV) The **1** In Word the beginning Became Flesh was the Word, and the Word was with God, and the Word was God. **2** He was with God in the beginning. **3** Through him all things were made; without him nothing was made that has been made.	Joh 1:1-3 New Living Translation (NLT) Prologue: Christ, the Eternal **1** In the Word begin-ning the Word already existed. The Word was with God, and the Word was God. **2** He existed in the beginning with God. **3** God created every-thing through him, and nothing was created except through him.

If God made everything, and He did, then how can we hate anything or anyone that He made? Or how can we believe that God who so loved the world that he gave his one and only Son, that **whoever** believes in him shall not perish but have eternal life, make some "whoevers" better than other "whoevers"?

Consider the definition of "white supremacy":

"noun

The belief, theory, or doctrine that white people are inherently superior to people from other racial and ethnic groups especially Black people, and therefore rightly the dominant group in any society."

Accepting the definition of white supremacy, I would like to suggest that the digital social media start a conversation/discussion on the extent of hate based on the following fictitious scenarios:

Scenario #1

Hey Mr. Bigot, can I please have a moment of your time today?

I'm starting a conversation but need to know first exactly how you pray.

Because I would imagine that in a certain type of situation, praying must cause you much consternation.

What if you pray for help after your car has flipped over, the doors won't open and there is a strong gasoline odor?

And, who would have known the decision you would endure when a Black man is the first responder God sent in response, your prayer to assure.

Do you tell God, 'no-thanks' to the one standing ready to extract you from your car with the Jaws-of-Life; the one standing right there ready to rescue both you and your wife?

Scenario #2

Well Mr. Bigot, maybe to this hypothetical story you have an answer.

Your close loved one has been suffering for months with a serious form of cancer.

You pray to God for mercy for there is nothing the doctors can do.

God replies I have sent you someone who can heal your loved one, but she happens to be a Jew.

Oh my, what is your reply? Please let me know Mr. Bigot, what would you do?

Scenario #3

Okay then Mr. Bigot, try this imaginary story on for size.

You are in desperate need of a lifesaving organ transplant and pray to God for a donor, when you suddenly realize, that you failed to specify in your prayer that you would not accept one from an ethnic group you despise.

Do you ask God for a 'do-over' prayer? while you wait for a more favorable answer with continued pain that you can no longer bear?

Is your hatred so deep-seeded that you could have the audacity to go to God and tell?

Would you risk spending the rest of your life in pain, which must be a living hell?

Scenario #4

Lastly, Mr. Bigot let's suppose you are in the military haven made an oath, your country to defend. You are ordered into combat and have a choice of who will protect you from the rear.

You choose three soldiers. Two men flee in fear.

The one God chose to save your life, is a combat expert that fights like a ferrous cheetah.

You want to thank God, but the soldier is Latina.

Do you tell God not save you again with a soldier who is a woman, especially one not of your ethnicity?

Such hate, and oh such a pity.

I'm sorry Mr. Bigot but I just don't understand, how you can dictate to God and you're only a man.

Instead of thanking God for sparing your life, you would rather continue to promote hate and strife?

If your religion makes you hate someone, you need a new religion.

Epilogue

A Digital Solution to a Difficult Dichotomy

8 Let no debt remain outstanding, except the continuing debt to love one another, for whoever loves others has fulfilled the law. 9 The commandments, "You shall not commit adultery," "You shall not murder," "You shall not steal," "You shall not covet," and whatever other command there may be, are summed up in this one command: "Love your neighbor as yourself." 10 Love does no harm to a neighbor. Therefore, love is the fulfillment of the law (Romans 13:8-10).

11 Don't speak evil against each other, dear brothers and sisters. If you criticize and judge each other, then you are criticizing and judging God's law. But your job is to obey the law, not to judge whether it applies to you. 12 God alone, who gave the law, is the Judge. He alone has

*the power to save or to destroy. So, what right
do you have to judge your neighbor (James
4:11-12 NLT).*

There are very few incidents involving firearms that have occurred that would not have had a more favorable outcome if the ammunition used had been digital. If our intent is simply to disable and not to kill, who could possibly object to a device that could temporarily incapacitate instead of "permanently" incapacitating.

Clearly most arm bearers are not intent on killing, but on defending or protecting. And the majority, I think, are God-fearing persons. I would like to believe, for example, that if I heard a noise in my home and turned on the lights to find a burglar, I could, in most states, legally shoot him. On the other hand, if I saw that the burglar was a scared teenager, I could just as easily call the police while holding my firearm on the suspect until law enforcement arrived. Just because I have a legal right to use my firearm doesn't mean that I must.

It is my belief that the technology available in the Digital Age can resolve the dichotomy of being able to worship God and keep His commandments, while still having the right to bear arms. There are many positive reasons for using digital ammunition. Here are a few:

➢ Greatly reduce the number of accidental firearm incidents in the home.

➢ Allow law enforcement to decide what situations warrant the use of non-lethal force.

➢ Commercial banks could determine if private security guards should be permitted to carry non-lethal firearms, in lieu of being unarmed as most of them are now.

➢ Small towns, municipalities and school districts could elect to have law enforcement

➢ and school security to routinely use non-lethal weapons and reduce liability insurance premiums significantly.

➢ Reduce the stress of decision making as to when to use deadly force in minor law enforcement and other situations as determined by law enforcement management.

➢ Police sharpshooters would have less stressful decisions to make in hostage situations, when time allows (standoff situations for example) for non-lethal action.

➢ Greatly reduce possible injury to innocent bystanders.

➢ Eliminate any excuse for anyone to use a firearm for lethal purposes, other than law

➢ enforcement personnel and the military.

➢ Judicial and jury decisions, as well as, prosecution charges would be made easier. If your intent is not to kill, you would use digital ammunition and would be charged accordingly. The use of non-digital ammunition by anyone other the military or law enforcement would be a criminal act to be adjudicated by the courts.

➢ Law enforcement morale would improve if officers were less likely to face severe

➢ disciplinary consequences for incidental lapses in judgement or, negative public perception.

➢ Help to bridge the divide between the public and law enforcement.

I have summarized this issue in the thought-provoking poem below:

The Right to Bear, Share and Care

An amendment and a commandment, how can they co-exist? The right to bear arms and the right to life are issues on which both consist.

The freedom of religion granted under the Constitution, the freedom to do God's will; with an added responsibility to obey the commandment, "Thou shall not kill".

We have the constitutional right to bear arms, but we also have a biblical responsibility to be free of anger and strife.

And in maintaining the right to bear arms, we must endeavor to do so without infringing upon another person's right to life.

Maybe the answer is not in arms, but with a different and creative type of ammunition; which could possibly be the only way to do away with the inevitable attrition.

It could stop some of the killing or being shot accidently in the head, with the mandatory use of smart bullets instead.

Except for the military and law enforcement, make smart ammunition available for any type of gun; thus, placing the responsibility on the owner to justify the need for an assault weapon.

It would also be their responsibility in a court of law, to prove their need for this type of protection. And a judge or jury would have to then decide on their punishment or sentence them to correction.

Sure, smart bullets will probably come with high initial production cost. And there still will most likely be an occasional life lost. But the truth is that all lives matter, and we need to stop all the debate and the un-necessary chatter.

Let us remember: "Life is short. Death is sure. Sin is the cause. Christ is the cure. For it was because of love that God sent his Son, of that we can be sure."

Smart bullets should have the ability to temporarily incapacitate, which would give God's creatures another chance at life, without pre-judging their fate; thus, avoiding mistakes at all cost, because it is His will that none of us should be lost.

While the unfortunate needless debate will still go on regarding the types of arms we can bear, at least we can curtail the killing occurring now as though we don't love or care.

How can we continue to say that we love God who we have never seen yet be so cruel to any of God's human beings...............? oh, how mean!

So, let those who wish to bear arms for their life and property to protect. But at the same time God's commandments must be given proper respect.

Who will invent smart bullets if they have not been invented already, I don't have a clue? But if I were an inventor, I know what I would do.

I would pray to the Lord for the wisdom, sci-entific knowledge and math. Trust Him with all my heart and allow Him to direct my path.

But until such time that smart ammunition becomes reality, what is it that God would require of you and me? The answer comes from the book of Micah, that we are to love mercy and walk humbly with God, how much plainer could that be?

Yet we continue to discuss and debate with seemingly every discussion laced with hate. And in the interim we continue to kill; with no answers still.

We can quote the Bible until we are blue in the face and hold up the Constitution for all to embrace.

But unless we can resolve this issue with love, we will not be able to please the Holy One above.

We will continue down a path of self-destruction where we are destined to dwell, a path that will sentence us to a life of living hell.

It is my sincere prayer that digital (smart bullets) will come to fruition, as an acceptable form of ammunition. That it might bridge the division and separation existing in our Nation, bringing about restoration and salvation.

May this dream of digital bullets become a reality and this land in which we trod, can become a nation with love for God.

A nation worshipping God in the Digital Age with the right to bear, share and care. Amen.

Parting Scripture

19 My dear brothers and sisters, take note of this: Everyone should be quick to listen, slow to speak and slow to become angry, 20 because human anger does not produce the righteousness that God desires. 21 Therefore, get rid of all moral filth and the evil that is so prevalent and humbly accept the word planted in you, which can save you.

22 Do not merely listen to the word, and so deceive yourselves. Do what it says. 23 Anyone who listens to the word but does not do what it says is like someone who looks at his face in a mirror 24 and, after looking at himself, goes away and immediately forgets what he looks like. 25 But whoever looks intently into the perfect law that gives freedom and continues in it—not forgetting what they have heard but doing it—they will be blessed in what they do.

26 Those who consider themselves religious and yet do not keep a tight rein on their tongues deceive themselves, and their religion is worthless.

27 Religion that God our Father accepts as pure and faultless is this: to look after orphans and widows in their distress and to keep oneself from being polluted by the world (James 1:19-27).

Glossary

Digital Devices include such devices as:

- Desktop computers - A computer designed for use by one person with no portability.
- Laptop computers - Also known as notebooks are portable computers.
- Mobile phones - A portable device used to make and receive wireless and/or land line telephone calls.
- Tablet computers - Ultra-portable compute smaller than a laptop.
- E-readers - Portable device that allows the user to read print books on a computer screen.
- Storage devices - A unit that stores all types of digital information.
- Scanners – A machine that can "read" bar codes and newer similar technology.

Smartphones – Mobile phones that incorporate calculator function, camera and other applications, in addition to texting capability and voice communication.

eBooks – Reading materials in digital format for reading on an e-reader device

Digital Television – A tv that can stream movies and shows from the internet, rather than just receive programs broadcast on air, cable or satellite.

Video Streaming – Watching movies or shows online or live shows.

Digital Music – Music that is streamed from the internet or purchased and downloaded to a digital device for listening.

Social Media – Enables users to interact with other users using text, photos and video.

Digital Camera – A modernized camera that replaces the traditional one that had to use film with one that has the capability to capture and store digital images.

About the Author

The author of this book is not a pastor, minister, deacon, elder, evangelist, theologian nor a biblical scholar. He is a Christian writer who simply loves the Word of God and shares what he has learned from the viewpoint of a worshippers' reading and study of the scriptures. This book is his second (the first, Worshipping God in an Imperfect Church), and is also written from the perspective of "a view from the pew". One view, from one worshipper's one pew, of many pews.

He writes to encourage readers to prayerfully study and examine the scriptures for themselves (in addition to hearing and learning from others) to gain a better appreciation and understanding of the Word of God.

Endnotes

1   https://www.facebook.com/lystra.elderstjohn/timeline?l-st=100003599263774%3A689172062 %3A1577424036

2   https://www.biblegateway.com/versions/Message-MSG-Bible/

3   Top 30 Quotes of Oscar Romero https://www.inspiringq-uotes.us/author/8967-oscar-romero

4   Culled from WhatsApp by Ike Onwubuya

5   https://www.facebook.com/cceva.org/posts/pope-fran-cis-wordsdo-you-want-to-fast-this- lentfast-from-hurt-ing-words-and-say-k/10155067619164732/

6   Mary Meeker's 2018 Internet Trends Report: All the slides, plus analysis.

7   Peterson, Cathy. Call Me If You Need Anything and Other Things Not to Say (back cover). Publisher: Chalice Press (April 1, 2005).

8   Hate Crimes Summary. 2018 FBI Hate Crimes Statistics, available on the FBI website.